Don't Throw Those Coupons Away! – A Mom's Guide to Saving Money at the Grocery Store
Copyright © 2010 by Kristin Peoples

ISBN 9780615355566

Printed in USA

Dedication

I give praises to God for giving me the vision to create this book. I dedicate this book to my children Devin, Kenneth II and Mychel. They are the loves of my life. I also dedicate the book to my husband Kenneth whose encouragement helped me complete the book. It is also dedicated to my parents, Clarence and Deanie whose love is always there. And also to my sister Kelley who shares my love for MJ.

Table of Contents

Preface

This book was developed out of necessity. Prices continue to rise at the grocery store. As a stay at home mom I had to find a way to feed my family.

I always knew about couponing but it was time to take it to the next level. It's so much more than cutting a few coupons out of the Sunday Paper. There is a true strategy to saving money with coupons. Once I discovered this I was able to cut my grocery bill in half.

Introduction

Everywhere you turn you hear about the economic downturn. People are losing their jobs and are left without the money they need for everyday necessities. There are some people who have taken jobs making substantially less in order to help them survive. Meanwhile, the price of food has not decreased. In fact, the prices are continuing to soar.

Grocery items are essential for each and every family. Those of us who have children know that you cannot just eat ramen noodles. Children and babies must eat to help them grow. The worst thing in the world for a Mom or Dad to hear is that their child is hungry and there is nothing they can do.

Coupons are what the manufacturer provides to help get their product into your home. There is no doubt that they are available to help the company build their business. But did you ever consider that coupons can help you decrease your grocery costs? Using coupons can help you get money off of the products you will buy anyway.

You may have heard about people who save a lot of money with coupons but may be confused as to how to actually do it. Most television segments show you only bits and pieces of what the 'Coupon Queen' did to save so much money. There wasn't a lot to go on. It can be a very frustrating process if you don't have all of the information to make it work for you.

Chapter One
Coupons Can Save Money

The economy is tough right now. All across the country, people are losing their jobs, losing their homes and trying to find ways to feed their families. In what is being called The Great Recession, many people are now finding that the foods they once enjoyed are now too expensive, and they need a way to put good food on their family's table.

When you want to save money for your family, but you want to do it in a way that is viable, legal and easy to do, then you should look at coupons. Coupons have been a saving grace for millions of people since they were first created in the late-1800s by the Coca-Cola Company. It was with Coca-Cola that employees and salesmen were encouraged to distribute coupons for Coca-Cola to customers. Coca-Cola would also mail coupons to customers and place them within magazines. This coupon policy essentially created Coca-Cola as we know it today, making the company successful. It is estimated that between 1894 and 1913, one out of every nine Americans had received a free Coca-Cola, which amounted to 8.5 million drinks

By 1909, coupons became widespread and currently over 700 corporations offer coupons that give discounts on various items and services. To show just how widespread coupon is use

Don't Throw Those Coupons Away!

is now, it is estimated that each year, $3 billion in transactions are done with the use of coupons.

Coupons are something that can help you when you need a helping hand. Every day, you can open up the newspaper and find a variety of coupons to entice you to buy. With coupons at the grocery store, you can literally save hundreds of dollars per month by shopping smart.

Coupons will come in many varieties in order to get your business to a store. Varieties include:

• Buy One, Get One Free: A common type of coupon in which you buy one product and get a second one free. If you buy a $10 box of hamburgers, you get a second one for free, thereby saving you $10 and giving you double what you would have bought initially.

• X% Off: Probably the most common form of coupon is the one that gives you a certain percentage off on your purchase. This will typically range between five and 40 percent. So, if you buy a $40 box of chicken breasts, then you will save between two dollars and $16 on that purchase. Another form of this is a coupon that saves you money on your total purchases. For example, this would be a coupon that says "Spend over $100 and you save 15 percent on your purchases!" So, you spend $100 and you pay $100, but if you get $101 in items, you only spend $85.85.

• Today Only: These coupons offer deals but only on a specific day. One thing many grocery stores do is offer 10 percent off your purchases on the first Tuesday of every month.

So, buy your $100 in items on Monday and you pay $100, but buy those items on Tuesday and you spend $90.

- Multiple Purchase Savings: This is a coupon type that is becoming common as well. With this type of coupon, if you buy one jug of milk you spend $2.50, but if you buy two jugs of milk you only spend $3.25. This saves you $1.75 and gives you an extra jug of milk.

There are truly multiple ways that companies will entice your business your business with coupons. Coupons are incredibly useful because they make your life easier. When you need to find a way to save $400 on your groceries each month, but to also eat healthy, coupons are your savior.

Coupons are the life-line in tough times that many people latch onto, and during good times they are great ways to save money for those bad times that always come down the road.

A Brief History of Coupons

As was mentioned earlier, the Coca-Cola bottling company was the first to begin using the concept of coupons, thanks to their handwritten tickets that provided free glasses of coke to customers. While this is the beginning of coupons for the world, it is by no means the only part of coupon history.

After Coca-Cola started with coupons, grocer C.W. Post (creator of Post Cereal) decided to try the same thing by giving one cent discounts on his breakfast cereal, Grape Nuts.

Don't Throw Those Coupons Away!

By the 1930s, coupons became widespread because of the need for cheap food when there were so many people starving. Coupons also helped businesses stay in business by ensuring customers still came into the businesses to buy things that they needed.

One of the biggest benefits for coupons came in the 1940s when supermarkets started to appear throughout the country. These supermarkets offered cheaper prices, but also used the concept of coupons that they took from the small grocery stores that were now being pushed out of business.

In the 1950s, coupons were become so widespread that the Nielson Coupon Clearing House was created for the purpose of coupon redemption. Created in 1957, this was the first company to base all its business around coupons and coupon redemption. Thanks to companies like this, half of all Americans in 1965 were using coupons and by 1975, roughly 35,000,000,000 were being distributed throughout the United States on a yearly basis. To show how often coupons were used, there were 215,000,000 Americans in 1975 and that means on average each American used 162 coupons per year. That is roughly one coupon for every second day of the year.

By 1997, 83 percent of all Americans were using coupons, which accounted for $2.9 billion savings for consumers. One of the biggest changes for coupons also came in the 1990s when coupons could be printed off the internet. Many internet retailers also jumped on board the coupon bandwagon through the use of

Don't Throw Those Coupons Away!

discount codes, key codes, promo codes, shopping codes and vouchers.

These coupons typically offered discounts and free shipping on orders from the website.

Some Coupon Facts

Coupons are a big part of our lives and there are some amazing facts associated with these simple pieces of paper that can save you a lot of money when saving money is vitally important to your life.

• Only 22 percent of consumers feel self-conscious about using coupons at the grocery store. Most consumers have no problem using coupons on a daily basis.

• Of the 22 percent who felt self-conscious about clipping coupons, 57 percent admit they do not feel as awkward now doing so during the current recession.

• Roughly 26 percent of consumers below the age of 35 have had their awkwardness related to coupons greatly reduced due to the economic recession.

• Of those who are having financial trouble, only 23 percent actually have a problem redeeming coupons.

• Roughly 40 percent of all people aged 35 to 54 have used coupons in the last six months.

• About 36 percent of consumers aged 55 to 64 have used coupons in the last six months.

Don't Throw Those Coupons Away!

- For individuals over the age of 65, only 25 percent have used coupons in the last six months.
- Currently, 79 percent of the American population uses coupons. With 309,000,000 Americans alive today, that means over 244,000,000 use coupons on at least a weekly basis.
- Through coupons, shoppers have saved over $3 billion.
- In a recent survey, about 69 percent of all shoppers have said they will often check and clip coupons as part of their shopping routine.
- Over half of all Sunday papers are purchased for the purpose of buying coupons.
- About 86 percent of women in the United States use coupons when they go shopping.
- About 69 percent of men in the United States use coupons when they go shopping.
- Educational background seems to have an impact on how often a person uses coupons. Roughly 73 percent of individuals who only have a high school diploma use coupons, while 80 percent of individuals with some college background use coupons. For individuals with college degrees, almost 80 percent use coupons. What is odd here is that people who only have high school often make much less than those who have a college degree. Hence, they should be the most likely to use coupons but a full seven percent less actually use coupons on a regular basis when you compare the two.

No matter your educational background, your sex, where you live, or what job you have, you will use coupons. Everyone uses coupons, even those with lots of money, because everyone wants to save money.

Don't Throw Those Coupons Away!

When you save money, you can put money elsewhere and that is very important during tough economic times. You should also not feel awkward when you use coupons because you are just one of 244,000,000 people who use coupons on a regular basis.

If anything, you should be proud of yourself because you have chosen to save money and be smart when you shop. Feeling awkward with coupons is not something you should worry about because you are saving money in tough economic times and that takes intelligence.

So, let's learn how you can save money with coupons.

Can I Feed My Family of 4, 5, 6 or More on $50 or Less A Week?

This may seem impossible, but it is not. You can truly feed your family for only $50 per week, and you do not have to buy food at the 99 cent store to do it. In fact, you can go and buy food for your family and only spend $50 through the power of coupons.

There are several things you can do to ensure you can meet the goal of only spending $50 a week, or $200 per month on food.

1. Do not go out to eat. If you do go out to eat, only eat at places that offer great discounts and coupons for your food.

Don't Throw Those Coupons Away!

Some restaurants allow children to eat free, which can save you half the cost of your food. As well, various nights are discounted on certain types of meals.

2. Cut out all the coupons that you can. If you bring coupons for most of the products you buy, you can easily turn a $100 a week grocery shop into just $50 or less per week.

With these three tips, you can easily cut down the amount you spend on food to help conserve money. Of course, there are other ways to save money including growing your own food in the garden and buying food at farmer's markets. These simple tactics help you save money and in tough economic times, the money you save can be used to pay your bills and even pay your mortgage.

Without coupons, this would not be possible. Coupons make it much easier to save money because they cut the costs of everything you buy. If you only buy items that have coupons associated with them, or on sale, you will save more than you ever thought possible.

Here is an example to show you just how this can be possible.

- If you do not use any coupons, you spend $100.
- If half the items you buy are half priced, then you save $25 and you only spend $75.
- If you shop on 10 Percent off Tuesday, you only spend $90.
- If you get 15 percent off when you spend $100 and above, you spend $85.

Don't Throw Those Coupons Away!

- If the average discount you get on all your items is 30 percent, then you only spend $70.
- If you shop on 10 Percent off Tuesday, and half the items you buy are half priced and the rest are averaging out at 20 percent off, then you only spend $54.

These are simple examples, but the last example shows how you can just spend $50 per week based on common coupons.

Ways to Make $50 Happen

There are a wide variety of ways that you can make $50 a week a part of your lifestyle, and it involves not just using coupons, but shopping right and shopping smart. The first thing you want to do is to make a list of the things you want to buy. One thing you can do here is to make your menu for the week so that you only buy what you need. Making your own menu also allows you to choose cheap foods but also healthy foods.

Always look for sales because the more sales you find, the more money you are going to save. Combining sales and coupons give you even more savings, and we will go into more detail on this form of coupon stacking later on in this book.

Some other tips include:

1. Know what you have on hand so you only buy what you need. Don't go to the store and try and remember if you need

peanut butter because you may not need any. Before you do your grocery shop, go through the cupboards, freezer and fridge to find exactly what you need. Do not buy what you do not need.

2. DO NOT, under any circumstance, shop when you are hungry. When you are hungry, going to the store to buy something as small as a loaf of bread can turn into a bunch of large purchases because you are hungry and thinking with your stomach, rather than your head.

Chapter Two
Introduction to Couponing

Coupons are the currency of tough times, and the crutch of people who want to save money when they are shopping for food and other items that they need. Of course, it is not just about coupons when you are trying to save money and you cannot just grab coupons on the day you go shopping to hope you find the deals you want. Couponing needs to be organized, concise and you need to be prepared with your couponing. In this chapter, we will show you just how you can do though through why you should coupon, how to organize your coupons and how to understand coupon lingo.

Saving Grocery Money for Other Expenses

For every one dollar you save on your groceries, which is one more dollar that you can put towards other expenses. For example, if you find that in the winter your heating costs go up drastically, you will want to cut back on other expenses. With the use of coupons, you can do this. If you spend $500 per month on your food each month, but then cut that down by 60 percent through the use of smart shopping and coupons, you will only spend $200 a month. This means you have $300 extra a month to devote to paying for the heat in your furnace.

Don't Throw Those Coupons Away!

Saving money on your groceries keeps your other expenses from getting out of control. The great thing here is that you are not sacrificing health or good food by cutting back on what you spend for groceries. With coupons, you are getting what you need to eat healthy, but you are saving money to keep you from falling into debt.

Coupons are the perfect solution to tough economic times.

Rain Checks

One of the most common problems that a coupon shopper runs into is when they go to get an item on sale and find out that it has already been snapped up by those before them. Amateur coupon shoppers will just buy another item, usually for more, because what they wanted is gone. However, smart coupon shoppers know about the power of the rain check. The rain check originated through baseball. When the game would be rained out, spectators would get a rain check assuring them that when the game was replayed, they would not have to buy another ticket. This concept has made its way into the retail world as well. These days, a rain check is most commonly knows as an extension of an offer and an assurance from a business to a customer that the customer can take advantage of a sale even after the sale has passed.

This means that if you go to the store for a half priced $25 turkey, but the turkeys are out, you can get a rain check. With the rain check, when those turkeys arrive again in a week or so, you will get half price, even if the sale is over. All you have to do for this is to talk to a manager.

The Retail Food Store Advertising and Marketing Practices Law

One thing that many coupon buyers do not realize is that the Federal Trade Commission made a law in 1971 which is called the Retail Food Store Advertising and Marketing Practices Law. This law is also called the unavailability rule and it protects you from grocery stores that want to advertise bargains to attract customers to their store, but who do not put out enough of the sale item to satisfy all the customers.

As a result of this law, the store MUST clearly state on the coupon or sale flyer that "quantities are limited" or that the product is "not available in all locations." If the coupons or sale flyer does not say either of these, and if you go to the store to find there are no products, the store MUST then do the one of the following:

1. Provide you with a rain check that allows you to buy the product at a later date for the sale price.
2. Provide you with a substitute product of comparable value (a different brand of apple juice from the brand that was advertised for example.)
3. Compensation that is at least equal in value to the value of the advertised item.

The rain check will usually be presented to you as some sort of voucher. It is typically an IOU voucher that the manager of the store will give you. This rain check can be done up professionally on ready-made paper, or it may be something as simple as the manager writing on a piece of paper that you are entitled to this product at a specific price. The manager cannot put an expiry on this, so if they do you should call them on it.

Make sure you hold onto the rain check because it can come in hand at a later date.

Rain Check Ideas

There are also some very important things to remember about rain checks. First, a rain check is a sale, not a coupon and that means you are allowed to combine it with manufacturer offers and coupons. You cannot redeem a rain check but the rain check can be used on another promotion for the same item. If in this regard the current sale price is higher, you can use the rain check IOU voucher you got from the store to pay the lower price. If the current sale price of the product is lower, then just hold onto the rain check voucher until later when the sale is over.

You should also not be afraid of stockpiling rain checks and using them when they are needed. There is nothing saying that you are not allowed to do this and grocery stores cannot prevent you from using the rain check in this manner.

Price Markdown

A price markdown is also something to watch for, and it can be tied in with a rain check. The price markdown is a reduction in the selling price of a product or service, and businesses will use it to increase the rate of sale of an article, often for clearance.

Markdowns are also used on products that are going to be obsolete, or if a new product is coming on the market in a different style. If a company changes its name or marketing strategy, then markdowns will be done to sell the old products. Finding the old products is a great idea because you can save a lot of money by looking for markdowns, on products that are perfectly fine.

Philanthropy

One aspect of getting coupons and deals that many coupon hunters look for is philanthropy. Philanthropy is when someone gives away good, money, or services and you can use this concept to your advantage.

Many companies will offer deals and donations for certain things, and you need to look for them. When you find them, you will be able to save even more than you thought you would have with coupons. Often, philanthropy will be through coupons that are to benefit others. For example, by signing up for a breast cancer awareness site, you may get a coupon for 10 percent off at your grocery store.

Chapter Three
Organization

Binders

One of the most common tools for organizing coupons is the binder. With a binder, you have a mobile coupon kit that can come with you so that you can get the coupons you need for where you are shopping. You want to have all your coupons with you because you will not miss out on any deals when you do this. Creating a coupon binder is very important, and here is how.

1. With a divider, you should split your coupons into categories. Since we are concentrating on food, you can have the following categories:

   a. Beverages
   b. Fruits
   c. Vegetables
   d. Perishables
   e. Canned Goods
   f. Pasta
   g. Desserts
   h. Baked Goods
   i. Meat
   j. Fish
   k. Chicken
   l. Breakfast

2.   Once you have created your categories, which should all be divided up with dividers. You can use baseball card protector sheets in each section to hold the coupons for that section.

3.   Sort all your coupons into the categories and file them in a way that helps you. A good way to file them is in alphabetical order.

The great thing about the coupon binder is you can take it with you and it keeps you completely organized when you are doing your shopping. A coupon binder is one of your best friends when you are trying to shop and save money through the use of coupons.

Envelopes

If you do not want to use a binder, you can go for the easy approach of envelopes. Envelopes work the same way the binder does, and that is to split up the coupons into categories. Each envelope will be a category like you saw above. The great thing about the envelopes is that you can take them with you easily and sometimes they are easier to manage in a grocery store than a binder. It is also a cheap solution since envelopes are a dime a dozen to buy.

Boxes

Another option is to put coupons in small boxes. This is not an option that allows you to take all your coupons with you when you go shopping, but it can keep your coupons organized at home. Then, when you go out shopping you go into each box to grab the coupons you need.

Like with envelopes, each box is going to correspond with the categories that we outlined above. Each of these categories will hold the coupons associated with those categories. One great thing you can do here is to have categories and then organize your coupons in envelopes within the boxes. Each envelope can be a letter of the alphabet. This gives you a great bit of organization that can make it much easier to find the coupons that you need.

Coupon Lingo

Here are some common terms that you may need to be aware of when dealing with coupons and the inevitable fine print.

- AC – After Coupon
- AR – After Rebate
- BOGO – Buy One Get One Free
- C/O – Cash Off
- CRT – Mail-in Rebate proof with cash register tape
- $/1 – Cents off when one item is bought

Don't Throw Those Coupons Away!

- $/2 – Cents off when two items are bought
- G1G1F – Buy One Get One Free
- DND – Do Not Double
- Double Coupon – The value of the coupon doubles at the register
- FAR – Free After Rebate
- Inserts – Coupon packets in the paper
- IP – Internet Printable Coupon
- GC – Gift Card or Gift Certificate
- MANU – Coupon Provided From Manufacturer
- MIR – Mail in Rebate
- NED – No Expiration Date
- NFN –No form needed for the refund offer
- OOS – Out of Stock
- OYNO – On Your Next Order
- POP – Proof of Purchase
- Qualifier – This is the items needed for the rebate
- RC – Rain Check
- SMP – Specially marked packages
- UPC – Bar code on the product
- WSL – While Supplies Last, No Rain Checks
- WYB – Another product free with purchase of this product

Chapter Four
Where to Find Coupons

To use coupons, you are going to have to find the coupons. The great thing is that companies want you to use coupons, so they are going to make coupons very easy to find. What sense does it make for a company to provide you with deals and coupons, but not actually give you an accessible way to find those coupons?

Newspapers

Probably the easiest place to get coupons is the newspaper, since companies will put most of their coupons in the paper, or as inserts within the newspaper. All you have to do is look for them.

While some of your coupons do come through in the pages of the paper, where you really want to look is in the inserts of the newspaper.

In the United States, three main companies provide advertising inserts. They are SmartSource, Vlassis and PGBrand Saver. Individual companies, like Wal-Mart for example, put in their own inserts that only feature their coupons and deals.

No Insert

It is not uncommon to open up your newspaper and to find that there are no inserts inside. Inserts can be misplaced when the paper is being put together, and they can accidently slip out during the delivery. Losing an insert is something that may happen to you at least once or twice a month and for a good coupon hunter, it can be a real pain.

That does not mean that you should just live with the missing insert and hope you get an insert next week. Here are some ways you can prevent yourself from being left out of the coupons.

- On the days where it is worth it to get the coupons, usually on a Sunday, it may be worth it to go and buy several newspapers to ensure you get all the coupons. Remember, one newspaper may have two of the three inserts, while another paper may have the insert you are missing. Spending five dollars on several newspapers is worth it when it can save you hundreds of dollars a month.
- Get some papers that are out of your local area. Some grocery chains will put other types of coupons in those areas. For example, if you live in a poorer area of the city, the newspapers you get will have coupons related to what people in poorer neighborhoods buy, while newspapers in richer areas may have different coupons. Getting newspapers out of your area allows you to get coupons to help you create a more diverse collection

of coupons, and it allows you to save more money at grocery stores, in and out of your area.

• You can talk to people you know who are not interested in clipping coupons. This way, you get free newspapers which makes saving money on coupons all the more sweeter. You can ask your friends, family and neighbors to save the papers so you can go through them for inserts and coupons.

• Recycle bins are a gold mine for finding newspaper inserts and coupons. Most people will throw away these things and you just have to take a look in the recycle bins to find the coupons that will make your life easier.

• Take a walk to some public places like parks, bus stations and coffee shops and you will find plenty of newspapers and inserts that you can use to save some money. Make sure that no one is using these papers and make sure that you are not taking something that may belong to a store when you grab an insert.

Coupon Forms

Another option for coupons is coupon forms that are provided by grocery stores in order to allow you to get savings on food. These forms typically follow along the lines of mail-in rebates or instant rebates, but you have to fill out the forms in order to get the deals.

These are not the most common types of coupons but they can get you bigger savings down the road. Typically mail-in rebates will save you a great deal of money, often as much as 50 percent.

Another form of coupon forms is the ones you fill out to become a privileged member of a store. These member coupons allow you to get savings on goods but only if you are a member. Typically you will receive a card that you present each time you buy food.

Product Packaging

Another great place for coupons is packaging from manufacturers. Sometimes coupons will be placed in unique areas, and you may not even know there are coupons there. Manufacturers put coupons on these areas to ensure that they get more business from you, so why not take them up on the offer and use the coupons they give you.

There are a variety of places that you can get the coupons from on packaging including the labels of canned foods, the lids of cans and caps on bottles, the cardboard covers on frozen and packaged foods, on paper wrapping around soap, coupons within packaging, like you may find in dog food and printed instructions found on personal care products.

The Entryway of Stores

One of the most common places to find coupons is the entryway to stores. Stores will put up all their coupons currently available for you to grab and use. The only problem with this type of coupon attainment strategy is that you cannot always plan what you are going to buy, and instead you choose what you will buy based on the coupons that are available at the entryway of the store. That all being said, it is still a great place to find some coupons when you have not been able to get the newspaper insert for that week.

Coupons by Mail

There are some places you can get coupons mailed to you from, with the two largest coupon sources being Coupons Inc. and Print & Mail, which will send you coupons in the mail for the retailers that you request.

This is a perfect source of coupons for people who do not have internet access. As well, when these coupons are sent to you, they are sent on FSI Verifiable paper, which allows the retailer to ensure that the coupons they are getting are completely legit and legal. Each year, retailers lose $500 million on fraudulent coupons and that makes some gun-shy with taking coupons you have printed off at home.

Coupon Trains

On the same concept of coupons through the mail is the coupon strange. This practice was very popular before the internet, and it is still popular throughout the United States.

Coupons that are not in your local paper can be difficult to find but you may want them, and that is where coupon trains come in. Some people need your coupons and you need theirs, so why not use coupon trains?

A basic coupon train involves about three to six members. With this type of coupon train, the conductor (first person on mailing list) puts 40 to 200 coupons into an envelope and they send out the coupons to the next person on the list. When you get the envelope, you can take coupons out but you must put in as many coupons as you took out. Therefore, if you took out 10 coupons, you must put in 10 coupons. At this point, you mail the envelope to the next person on the list. Each person has the envelope for about one to three days and whoever has the envelope will take out any coupons that have expired.

Reasons for Coupon Train

There are several reasons people join coupon trains.

1.   When people have different needs and wish lists, they will benefit from a coupon train. For example, if someone needs baby coupons, another needs personal care coupons and another person needs pet coupons, all will benefit from the coupons put into the envelopes. If you need baby coupons, you take those out and you put in pet coupons because you do not need those, but someone else might.

2.   Coupon trains also benefit those who have similar needs. Many people need coupons for food, cleansers and baby products, and coupon trains help them. Many coupon trains are "Baby Only" or "Food Only" so you know exactly what you are getting with the coupon train.

Don't Throw Those Coupons Away!

3. Many coupon train participants will put a wish list in the envelope of their top 10 coupons so that they can get exactly what they need in the coupon train when it comes back to them.

Getting Manufacturer Coupons

In order to get manufacturer coupons, there are several things that you can do. Remember, manufacturer coupons can be combined with store coupons to create a huge wealth of savings for you.

The first thing you can do is to look through the newspaper for manufacturer coupons. The coupons provided from manufacturers are typically good for about two week to three months and if you can combine a manufacturer coupon with a store coupon during a store sale, you can literally spend next to nothing on the product you are buying.

Check out the websites of manufacturers, but also look at other websites like www.thecouponmaster.com and www.thecouponclippers.com. This is often a preferred method among people who want to get manufacturer coupons because they can get more than one type of coupon. For example, it is possible to get several exact coupons for one product, which can then be used at different stores, thereby allowing you to bulk up on the product.

One of the best ways, albeit rarely used ways, of getting manufacturer coupons is to actually call the manufacturer directly. All you have to do is call the 1-800 number that the manufacturer provides to get the coupon that you need. For a good list of manufacturer contact numbers, you can visit www.grocerycouponguide.com. This is not a perfect method by any means because it is estimated that manufacturers send coupons to about 30 percent of the customers who request them.

Online Auction Coupons

Amazingly, you can get your coupons from places like eBay.com, which allows you to get coupons from others. Selling coupons is illegal, but the people who "give away" coupons on eBay do so by charging a fee for the energy to find, clip and sort the coupons and send them to you. They are not selling the coupons, but they are selling their time to get the coupons for you.

If you are very busy, this can be a very good option because it gets someone else to find the coupons for you. However, if you are spending money to get coupons, you are often defeating the purpose of the coupons.

When you are using auctions to get coupons, make sure you know the exact coupon brand you need because there are thousands of coupon auctions going at this time. Input the brand name into eBay and you will find plenty of coupons that you can get, without even needing the Sunday paper.

Online Coupons to Print

The internet has really opened up the world of coupons to allow individuals to go online to get coupons, rather than having

Don't Throw Those Coupons Away!

to get coupons from the paper. In addition, some stores offer special coupons that are only found online, which means going online for coupons is a great way to gain some extra savings that others may not know about.

There are places you can go to get online coupons for your area that you can then print off and use in the store.

• Store websites: Whether it is Walmart.com, or another website for a grocery store you go to, you can get coupons from the website of the store you are planning at shopping at. Some of these stores even have special sections devoted to coupons, as well as printable flyers.

• You can also visit websites that are devoted strictly to providing coupons to its users. Some websites require you to join, but when you do you get more savings and even e-mail alerts when new deals come about. Some websites to visit include:

   o   http://www.fabuloussavings.com/online-usa-coupons/
   o   http://www.myretailcodes.com/
   o   http://www.shopping-bargains.com/

Grocery Store Links

If you want to find some extra coupons, or you want to check out the online deals offered through your grocery stores, then visit these websites:

• Costco: http://www.costco.com
• Wal-Mart: http://www.walmart.com

Don't Throw Those Coupons Away!

- Delhaize: http://www.delhaizegroup.com/
- Kroger: http://www.kroger.com/
- Piggly Wiggly: http://www.pigglywiggly.com/
- Safeway: http://www.safeway.com
- Sam's Club: http://www.samsclub.com/
- SuperValu: http://www.supervalu.com/
- Target: http://www.target.com/
- Whole Foods: http://www.wholefoods.com/

Chapter Five
Stockpiling

Stockpiling anything can be a good idea. People stockpile food to ensure that when food is scarce, they have something to eat. Well, the same works true with coupons. You stockpile coupons so that when you need them, you have them. You want to ensure you have coupons saved up because you may not use the coupons from that week's paper, on that week. Other coupons online may not come into effect yet, so you have to hold onto them.

To stockpile coupons for the purpose of stockpiling food, just do the following:

1. Get all the coupons that you want and put them on the table so that you can sort them easily. You will want to clip out all the coupons and arrange them in terms of categories, expiry and alphabetic positioning so that you can find them easily.
2. Pile the coupons according to the product and make sure you look at the expiry dates so you do not try and use expiry dates.
3. Go through the newspaper and look for advertisements that include coupons, or which announce sales that you should be aware of. Cut out the advertisements and circle the relevant part of the advertisement so you know what you are looking for.
4. With a pen and paper, write down a list of:

Don't Throw Those Coupons Away!

a. The stores you want to go to
b. The items you want to purchase at each store
c. The number of coupons to use at each store.
d. The price you expect to pay for everything at the store.
5. Total up how much you plan to buy with the non-coupon rate and the rate you will pay with your coupons so you can see how much you will save.

Now, you can keep all your coupons saved up for a specific day but you have to make sure that you do not have any expired coupons. You can have the coupons arranged for when they expire so you know when the coupons will be about to become worthless so you can use them.

Doing all this means that when you buy your food and other products at the store, you are going to be stockpiling your food because sometimes you may want to buy five boxes of cereal for the price of two, even though it will take you three months to get through those boxes. Stockpiling food also means you spend less on food because buying in bulk will save you money in the long run and help you always have good food in your belly.

Things to Remember With Stockpiling

1. Always know what you want to stockpile on. It does you not help you to stockpile on things you do not need. If you do, you are only wasting space within your stockpile pantry.
2. Use vouchers, promos and sales to stockpile up on items. This gives you more for what you spend.

3.   Buy as many items as you can at the lowest price. If this means buying 15 packages of toilet paper, do it. You won't have to buy toilet paper for a year and that is money you now save. It could save you hundreds of dollars a year to do this.

Stockpiling Food

To stockpile food in your home, do the following:

1.   Have a spot in the home that is designated for food. It needs to have a lot of shelving so a pantry or closet will work great.

2.   Organize all the items together so you can inventory them. Having an inventory list lets you know when you are getting low on something.

3.   Always pay attention to the shelf life of your products so nothing goes bad. If something goes bad, you are only wasting money.

When you stockpile food, you are preparing for times when you may not have money for food.

Think about the story of the ants and the grasshopper. The ants stockpiled food, worked hard and made sure they had food for the winter while the grasshopper didn't. When winter came, the grasshopper had no food, and the ants were able to relax with a large store of food to go to.

Chapter Six
Coupon Strategy

When you are working with coupons and trying to save money with coupons, you want to make sure you have a strategy. Having a coupon strategy is very important because it allows you to get the most savings and the most bang out of the money you are spending. If you just go to the store without stopping to organize your coupons, or have a strategy, you will miss out on deals and on savings that could help you. Remember, every dollar that you save on your groceries is a dollar you can spend elsewhere. Saving money saves you stress over financial situations, and it is important to never forget that.

Coupon Combinations and Matching Sales

One of the best strategies that you can have with coupons is to be able to combine them. When you combine coupons on an item, you are getting a double hit of savings and it is all perfectly legal. For example, if you go to the store and there is toilet paper listed at $15 for a 20 rolls. Thankfully, you have a coupon that gives you half price on the 20 rolls so now you are only paying $7.50. However, you also see that there is a mail-in rebate on these rolls, which gives you $10 back if you send the rebate in. This means that while you initially pay $7.50 for the rolls, you end up being paid $2.50 because you sent in the mail-in rebate. Here is how this combo breaks down:

Initial Price:	$15
Coupon:	50% off
New Price:	$7.50
Pay at Cashier:	$7.50
Mail-in Rebate Value:	$10
Total Paid for Item:	$7.50 - $10 = (-$2.50)

That is how easy coupon combinations can work for you and how much money you can save. By combining sales, refunds, rebates and more, you can not only save on the groceries but actually get more money back than what you paid for the item. We will address rebates in more detail in the next section.

In regards to matching sales, this can also save you a lot of money because of how companies work their sales and coupons. When you match sales, you are using the strategy of using coupons with a sale. Often a coupon will overlap with a sale, at the beginning of the life-cycle of the coupon, or the end of the coupon cycle. By this we mean that the last few days of a sale may fall on the first few days of a coupon offer, or vice versa. The reason for this is that stores will often put items on sale about one month after the coupon has been published, which allows the two to overlap. So, you do not want to use your coupons too early if you do not have to.

Don't Throw Those Coupons Away!

Here is an example to help you understand where we are coming from with this.

Electronics Warehouse is having sends out coupons in the Sunday paper that give you 10 percent off any high definition television in the building. You have your eye on a 47 inch plasma television, which costs $2,342. If you use the coupon now, you will save $234.20 and only spend $2,107.80. However, you also learn from someone you know at the store that the company is having a sale in three weeks, four days before the coupon expires, in which all plasma televisions are 30 percent off. So, you decide to save your coupon and by doing so you not only save $234.20 on the original coupon, but you also then save an additional 30 percent on the $2,107.80 new price. That gives you an additional savings of $632.34, which means you only spend $1,475.46 on a television originally costing $2,342. By combining a coupon and sale together, you received savings of 37 percent.

Chapter Seven
Rebates

Something that can save you a lot of money, but which many people do not take the time to use, is rebates. Rebates, especially mail-in rebates, are under-utilized but the savings they can provide are immense.

Essentially, a rebate is an amount that is paid back to you through a return, reduction or refund of what you originally paid. Instant rebates exist, but the most common form of rebate is the mail-in rebate. With the mail-in rebate, you send in a coupon, receipt and barcode to the company that makes the product you bought and you will receive a check back for the amount you paid.

The benefits to you are immense because of the lower pricing. Rebates are essentially a company paying you money to buy the stuff they make and all you have to do is ask them for the money. What is amazing is that so few people ever use mail-in rebates. According to Business Week, mail-in rebates have a return rate of about 60 percent, but some rebates are only having a two percent return rate. For example, in 2005, TiVo offered its subscribers a $100 mail-in rebate, but less than 50 percent actually took advantage of this.

The mail-in rebate works as follows:

1. You go to the store and find an item that you want to buy, a toaster for example.

2. You see there is a mail-in rebate on the toaster for $30. The toaster costs $50, so you have over 50 percent savings on the toaster if you use the mail-in rebate.

3. You buy the toaster and you keep the receipt. You also cut the bar code off the box.

4. You put the receipt and bar code in the box with the mail-in rebate offer in an envelope.

5. The company receives this and sends you a check for $30 as part of the mail-in rebate.

6. You put the $30 you receive in the bank and you end up only paying $20 for a $50 toaster.

Types of Rebates

The first type of rebate is the cash back rebate, as has been discussed above. These work just how the name suggests, you get money back on your purchase and there are two types of these; mail-in and instant rebates.

However, recently there is a new type of cash back rebate that companies are using. This type of rebate uses many items together to create a combo cash back rebate that requires all the items in the rebate to be purchased at the same time. For example, you would have a rebate that give you five dollars back on bacon, eggs and bread from one company but you have to buy all three at once to get 50 percent off. The problem here is that if there are no eggs, just bacon and bread, you do not collect on the rebate. Another form of this rebate is the one that requires you to buy multiples of an item to get cash back on it. An example of this is orange juice that gives you four dollars back but only if you buy three or more of the orange juice. If you only buy one, you do not get any cash back rebates.

The next type of rebate is the Try-Me Free rebates. These are different types of rebates that allow you to check out a new product and use it for a period of time for free. This is typically used for services like a 30-day free subscription to satellite radio so it does not apply for grocery shopping. However, there are some that do apply to grocery shopping and this includes submitting a survey to the company to get money back so they can see how much you liked the product. If you didn't like the product, you get your money back, which brings us to our next type.

The taste guarantee refund means that if you are dissatisfied with a product that you have tried, like cereal, you can get your money back by calling the company and stating that you were not happy with the product. Sometimes the company will give you money back, or give you coupons for free products. You will also have to submit your receipt and the UPC of the product. It is also important to note that this only works once and you cannot try and get free products from the company by continually saying you didn't like their product as they will get wise to the entire situation.

Don't Throw Those Coupons Away!

Rebate Tips

• Make copies of all documents that you send to the rebate center. If your rebate is lost, you do not want to be left without your rebate.

• Always check up on your rebate by calling the number provided on the rebate.

• You should receive your rebate within eight to 12 weeks, but check in on your rebate by calling the rebate center three weeks after you send the rebate off.

• Take advantage of sales and specials that offer rebates because you can save so much money doing so.

• Make sure that your rebate has not expired. Sometimes rebates will expire and you may forget about them. When you buy the product, you may have a rebate that has already expired because stores do not take rebate products off the shelf. The last thing you want is to buy a product and then find out that the rebate has expired because now you have spent more than you needed to.

• As with anything, you want to read the fine print. Read the fine print because if you do not read the fine print, you may end up paying more than you thought. Some things that the fine print will tell you include that you can only have one rebate per household, that you cannot purchase more than one of the item and that you have to purchase a certain other product to get the rebate on this product.

Chapter Eight
The Check Out

When you get to the check out, do not just dump all your coupons on the cashier. Your coupons should not be a jumbled pile, they should be organized. If they are not organized at the check out, you may find that some of your coupons get lost in the shuffle.

Store Feedback

Many stores have feedback forms that you can write down your experience with the store. This is also a great strategy with your coupons because not only can you explain how you would prefer the store coupons to work, but you can also get free items for your feedback. Either through sending a letter to the company that explains your experience with the company, or just filling out a form, you can get money off on your purchases for helping the store become better at serving its customers.

Couponing Tips

To make sure you have the best coupon strategy, try some of these great tips to ensure you get the most bang for your buck.

Don't Throw Those Coupons Away!

• Sign up for samples from the companies you shop with, as this can provide you with free food and some great coupons.

• Go to places like Coupons.com to print off coupons and sometimes you can print off more than one coupon to get more savings.

• Match your coupons with items on sale in the store. You will see plenty of tags sticking out saying "SALE!" and if you can match your coupon with that, you create a double hit of savings.

• Look inside the products you buy so that you can find any coupons that may be inside the packaging. Many companies offer rebate within the packaging but you have to look for them.

• Go to grocery store websites and find e-coupons that can provide you savings, especially if you have a member card that the savings can be put on.

• Find grocery stores that double coupons. Some stores allow this and it can save you a lot of money. If you have two coupons that save 25% off, then by doubling these coupons up you can get 50% off. For a list of stores that allow double coupons, you can visit this website: http://couponing.about.com/od/groceryzone/a/doublecoupons.htm

• You should save all your coupons and if there are coupons that you do not need, trade them with friends who may need them. There are actually many groups that meet these days to trade coupons and you can find a lot of coupons that you may need, but others do not, thereby saving you more money.

• If you can, try and plan out your menu so that you only buy what you need, and there are no impulse items. You do not want to buy on impulse because you will only lose savings that way.

Don't Throw Those Coupons Away!

- Know what is on sale so that you can stack coupons. This is essentially matching sales, but if you know when specific products are on sale, you can hold onto special coupons to make sure that you come out on top with savings.

What Not To Do

Mistakes do happen and when mistakes happen with coupons, you pay more than you need to. Follow these tips to know exactly what you should not do when you are couponing.

- Make sure you learn the policies of the store before you coupon. One of the biggest mistakes is to have coupons ready and when you get to the cashier you find out that your coupons are not valid in such a manner and now you are forced to pay full price, when you do not want to pay that much. A good example of this is to find out if the store allows you to double-up on coupons. If you are at a store that allows double-upping on coupons and you do not double-up, you do not save money.

- Using coupons without having a sale to go with them can also be a big mistake as we have already discussed. Hold onto your coupons if you think a sale is coming up so that you can increase your savings immensely.

- Even with coupons, you should compare the prices of retailers. You may get $10 off on toilet paper at one store, but if another store sells that toilet paper for $10 less as a regular price, then you should shop with the other store. However, you can also get the one store to play off the other and get $10 savings, plus the $10 discount. Many stores will beat a rival stores price, and honor your coupon to get your business.

Don't Throw Those Coupons Away!

- Forgetting to use a coupon on the buy one, get one free offers is also a mistake. When you use a coupon on this type of purchase, you buy one and get one free, plus you save money on the one you bought. If the cereal is buy one and get one free and you have a coupon for 20 percent off that cereal, then you can buy one cereal box for 20 percent off and then get another one free.

- Many stores offer reward cards and you should use reward cards in order to get extra savings beyond just using a coupon. Some cards provide you certain money back on your purchases. If you get five percent off on your purchases and you use coupons, you can actually spend significantly less than you ever thought possible. Forgetting about reward cards through stores is a big mistake novice coupon enthusiasts make.

It is very important that you have a good coupon strategy because you want to ensure that you get the most out of your coupons when you go shopping. If you fail to plan ahead, you do not get all the savings you could possibly get and that is essentially throwing money out the window.

Seasonal Sales Cycles

A very important part of the coupon strategy is the understanding the seasonal sales cycles of stores. Remember, you can combine coupons and sales to greatly increase your savings, and seasonal sales let you plan your coupon strategy properly.

48

Don't Throw Those Coupons Away!

An example of this is companies will offer sales on fruits and vegetables when they are in season, rather than out of season, because they cost less for the companies at that point. Typically vegetables and fruits will cost as much as three to five times as much out of season as they do in season.

Fruits and vegetables will be on sale when they are in-season, rather than when they are out-of-season. Ice cream and cold desserts are typically cheaper just before the summer season comes along, as well as when it is in the off-season. The best thing you can do is think of when something is most popular and often least-available, and that is the time when it is the most expensive. When the product is not as popular, and there are lots of supplies, the food will be cheaper. It all comes down to supply and demand. When there is a great demand, but limited supply, prices are high. When there is limited demand but great supply, prices will be lower and sales/coupons will be much more common.

Holidays are very common times when stores will have sales on food and products. An example of this is turkey before Christmas, but also directly after Christmas as well. Another common practice that works with sales cycles is when a manufacturer is issuing a new product. The manufacturer will typically buy shelf space at a store in order to push their new product. Shelf space is very expensive, so manufacturers will have sales on their products in stores in order to free up the space on the shelves for their new product. When you know a company is issuing a new product, go to the store and you should find big savings on their old product.

Don't Throw Those Coupons Away!

Here is an example of how this works. An apple juice supplier is putting out their new organic brand and they are no longer making their previous non-organic brand. To have the apple juice out in time for the spring season, the company puts a big sale on their previous apple juice product to sell it in time to get the organic apple juice out for sale by spring.

It can be very hard to find these savings if you do not know exactly what to look for. It is very important that you pay attention to trends. An example of this would be to know that ice cream manufacturers issue new blends of their ice cream just before the summer season, so they will often have sales on their product just before summer starts. Some more examples of sales cycles are listed below.

Just like when a company is trying to get rid of an old product they will have a sale, when the company is issuing a new product they will also have sales. Many companies have launch promotions on new products and will offer clearance prices in order to see what the customer response is to the product. If the customer response to the product is highly favorable, then the price will go up as a result.

When a company is issuing out new packaging, they will charge less to push the old product as well as to push the new packaging. Examples of times when companies will have new packaging, which you can capitalize on greatly after the holiday is over are Easter, Halloween, Christmas, Thanksgiving, during the Super Bowl, during the Olympics and more. The last few are true for when party snacks are popular, like chips, pop and junk food. Think of how much is bought for Super Bowl parties and

Don't Throw Those Coupons Away!

you will begin to see the amazing deals being offered during that time of the year.

Another time when sales are big is when it is the products month, week or day. For example, there is a National Peanut Month, and during that month the sales on peanuts are quite large to celebrate this. Keep an eye on certain events and you will actually find that there are several sales to correspond with these events. For example, the Westminster Dog Show will often happen at the same time as deals on pet food. Back to School season will give you more savings in August on lunch food and sandwich supplies. The July 4 long weekend will have sales leading up to it that push junk food, snacks and barbecue items. Halloween has sales on candy and pumpkins, while baking supplies are much cheaper during the Christmas season. You will even find eggs are cheaper during March and April in the lead up to Easter.

Below you will find a quick rundown of what items typically have coupons issued for them based on the month:

JANUARY

- Diet foods
- Healthy Choice
- South Beach
- Lean Cuisine
- Yogurt
- Cold Medicines
- Oatmeal
- Pepsi

Don't Throw Those Coupons Away!

- Coke
- Chips
- Dips
- Cheese
- Sandwich Food
- Crackers
- Snacks

FEBRUARY

- Canned vegetables
- Canned fruits
- Canned tuna
- Canned beans
- Cherry pie filling
- Cereals
- Waffles
- Low cholesterol items
- Dog food

MARCH

- Frozen vegetables
- Frozen fruits
- Frozen dinners/meals
- Ice cream
- Waffles
- Eggs
- Ham
- Asparagus

Don't Throw Those Coupons Away!

- Horseradish
- Butter
- Coconut
- Peanuts
- Potatoes
- Corned beef

APRIL

- Eggs
- Ham
- Asparagus
- Butter
- Coconut
- Marshmallows
- Cookie mix
- Sugar
- Powdered sugar
- Brown sugar
- Brownie mix
- Cake mix
- Food coloring
- Dyes
- Spices
- Horseradish
- Organic food

Don't Throw Those Coupons Away!

MAY

- Condiments
- Grilling meats
- Cheese
- Produce
- Potato chips
- Popsicles
- Hamburger Buns
- Hot dog buns
- Soda
- Salsa
- Tortillas
- Tacos
- Dog food
- Cat food

JUNE

- Milk
- Eggs
- Juice
- Cheese
- Butter
- Yogurt,
- Sour cream
- Cream cheese
- Ice cream
- Condiments
- Grilling meats

Don't Throw Those Coupons Away!

- Produce
- Potato chips
- Popsicles

JULY

- BBQ Sauce
- Baked beans
- Ketchup
- Mustard
- Mayonnaise
- Hot dogs
- Hamburger
- Ribs
- Steaks
- Buns
- Soda
- Blueberries

AUGUST
- Lunch Foods
- Pudding cups
- Lunch meat
- Bread
- Cold cereal
- Waffles

SEPTEMBER

- Pudding cups

Don't Throw Those Coupons Away!

- Juice boxes
- Pop Tarts
- Lunch meat
- Bread
- Cold cereal
- Waffles
- Spaghetti Sauce
- Tomato soup
- Canned tomatoes
- Tomato sauce
- Candy
- Cookies
- Baking chocolate chips
- Apples
- Pumpkins

OCTOBER

- Candy
- Cookies
- Chocolate chips
- Fruitcake
- Fruit nuts
- Apples
- Pumpkins

NOVEMBER

- Hot cocoa
- Coffee
- Tea

- Canned foods
- Baking goods
- Turkey
- Pumpkin
- Stuffing mix
- Potato mix
- Butter
- Sweet potatoes
- Fresh potatoes
- Gravy
- Bread/rolls
- Frozen pies

DECEMBER

- Cold cuts
- Sour cream
- Crackers
- Soda
- Ham
- Stuffing mix
- Potato mix
- Butter
- Fresh potatoes
- Gravy
- Bread/rolls
- Frozen pies
- Green beans
- Fried onion

- Cream soups
- Broth
- Pie filling
- Egg Nog
- Flour
- Sugar
- Butter
- Cream
- Cake mix
- Brownie mix
- Muffin mix
- Breads
- Pie Crust
- Marshmallow
- Whipped cream

Getting Free Items

Getting free items is very important to couponing because anything you get for free is money you have saved. Think of how great it would be if you can get ten rolls of toilet paper but only pay for five. That adds up to big savings!

The first thing you need to do to get free items at the grocery store is to stockpile your coupons. Go through all your newspapers, magazines and into the stores to grab coupons that will allow you to stockpile them and stack them. Once you have all your coupons, begin clipping them out. You can also print them off websites. The more coupons you have, the more things you will get for free.

Don't Throw Those Coupons Away!

Now, you want to look at the sales going on at the stores and match up the sales with the coupons. This will allow you to not only get free items, but save about 30 percent on all your other groceries.

When you have all your coupons, try and combine the coupons with frequent shopper cards. If you shop at one place over and over, then get a frequent shoppers card that you can use to get deals on everything. Many of these cards will give you 10 percent off your purchases. Before going further, we are going to show you how you can get things for free by combining these cards, coupons and sales.

So, you get 10 percent off all your purchases with your card. Now, you find four products in the paper that have coupons for $4 off each item. The items cost $7.99, $5.99, $5.99 and $6.99. In addition, you go to the store on the first Tuesday of the month and therefore save another 10 percent. This is how it breaks down.

- Pre-sales, coupon and card total price: $26.96
- Ten percent off card: $24.26
- Ten percent off for the sales day (on $26.96): $21.57
- $5 off each item (4 x $4)
  $5.57

So, you only spend $5.57, which is the cost of one of the items you bought. This essentially means you got the other four items for free!

Don't Throw Those Coupons Away!

You should also contact the manufacturers for samples. Manufacturers are quite open about sending free samples of the product for you to try. The products you receive may be smaller than the typical variety you find at the store, but any amount of items you get for free can help you save money. Always contact the customer service department when looking to get samples of the new products that the company is releasing as well.

One thing that is not often used is bartering. This will not work with the larger grocery stores, but if there is a locally-owned grocery store, you can use coupons, sales cards and the sale themselves along with bartering. Bartering will get the price down before you buy anything and it can save you a lot of money. Being friends with the manager can also help you save money and get items for nearly nothing. You can also exchange your services for items at the store. For example, if you are a plumber or electrician, you can offer your services for items at the store. Perhaps four hours of work is worth $150 worth of groceries at the store.

Lastly, if you want to get something for free from a grocery store, then the importance of Buy One Get One Free cannot be understated. Find these coupons wherever you can and use them as much as you can.

If you can combine coupons with these Buy One Get One Free, then all the better. For example, if you have a Buy One Get One Free on a $4.00 tube of toothpaste, then you are already saving $4.00 but you can go further. So, you use your shopper's card, and you use the sale day at the store. That means you save 20 percent on the purchase. Now, you get one free item and you

Don't Throw Those Coupons Away!

only spend $3.20. Now, if you can combine a manufacturer's coupon with that, and you get 20 percent off, then you are now only spending $2.56. If you have a coupon that also gives you $2 off hygiene purchases, you only spend $0.56 for two tubes of toothpaste valued at $8.00.

Chapter Nine
Drug Store Strategy

How It Differs From Grocery Stores

Grocery stores often make their money through coupons. With coupons, these stores are able to entice people to buy from them because coupons bring customers in. It is a way of spending money to make money, where as it is instead losing money to make money. Many people who occasionally use coupons will continue to shop at a store, even if they are not using coupons because they like the store.

This is why grocery stores use coupons so much.

Drug stores are a bit different. Drug stores are not as caught up in using coupons because they know that people will have to buy from them when they need medication, so there is not always a need for coupons. This does not mean that the drug stores do not use coupons, because they do, but a different strategy is often needed to ensure that you can get the most out of shopping at a drug store. Remember, you want to save money, and that can be hard if you do not know how to save money at a drug store.

Even though there are differences, you can still get some savings in the Sunday inserts and you can also get savings from the manufacturers. This is probably the best way to save money using coupons with drug stores because you can save money with the manufacturer rather than the store.

Register Rewards and the Walgreens Program

Walgreens is the largest drug store chain in the United States and if you are shopping at a drug store, you are most likely shopping at one of the 7,147 Walgreens located across the United States.

One reason why Walgreens is so popular is based on the fact that they offer some amazing deals through their Register Rewards program.

The Register Rewards program is a rebate system that uses instant rebates rather than mail-in rebates. This means you get instant savings at the cashier, rather than a check sent to you through the mail. Only certain items are marked by the Register Rewards program and each week the items are listed in the weekly sales flier that Walgreens sends out. The program works by giving you a coupon that prints out at the register that provides you a discount on your future purchases. Here is an example to help you understand the process:

You look in the Walgreens Flyer and you find a bottle of shampoo that is listed at $5.99 and it offers a $2.99 Register Rewards rebate on the product. So, you go to the store and you buy the shampoo and pay $5.99 for it at the register. The receipt prints out and with it comes a Register Rewards coupon that is worth $2.99 that can be redeemed on your next purchase. So, you go to the store within two weeks to buy another bottle of shampoo and you can use this instant rebate and only pay three dollars for the $5.99 shampoo bottle.

Some things to remember about this program is that it cannot be used on any tobacco or alcohol products, and the coupons expire two weeks after you receive them.

Rewards Program Tips

1. Spend as little as you can in order to save as much money as possible. You want to keep your out-of-pocket costs as low as you possibly can when you use the program. Combining coupons with your Register Rewards coupons is a good idea that can even bring you money back.

2. Look at the details of the product to ensure you do not accidently buy something that is not part of the Register Rewards program. If the Register Rewards program offers rewards on Crest Mint Toothpaste, then you should only buy that brand of toothpaste, not Crest Cherry Toothpaste because the rewards will not apply.

3. Use manufacturer coupons with your Register Rewards to get as much savings as possible.

4. If you use multiple transactions you can get even more savings. For example, if you are buying two shampoo bottles, you will only get one set of Register Rewards. However, you can easily ask the cashier to do two transactions on the two shampoo bottles, thereby getting two sets of Register Rewards.

Don't Throw Those Coupons Away!

Maximizing Savings with This Strategy

The first time you go into Walgreens, you will want to spend at least $15. This will give you a good base of Register Rewards that you can begin to use week after week. Each week, you will look for different deals and you will use the rewards that you received the last time you went shopping. This allows you to purchase items for free using the rewards you got the previous week. You can have the Register Rewards for two weeks, so you can wait a week to see what new deals are available. Each time you buy from Walgreens, hold over the Register Rewards, you get more and more free items. Some items you may not need at the time, but if you are getting them free it can be good just to grab them. Yes, you have plenty of mouthwash, but will you in four weeks? If you can get a free thing of mouthwash now, why not do so, then you don't pay later for that same mouthwash when your Register Rewards have expired.

Some other strategies to use include:

1.   You cannot use two manufacturer coupons on the same product. So, if you are buying toothpaste that has $2.00 off, you will not be able to use the Register Reward with it. Remember this so that you do not screw up your Walgreens strategy.

2.   Walgreens will not give you money back when you use coupons or Register Rewards, so do not expect to get money back if you have $10 off on an eight dollar mouthwash. This is very important because if the balance is -$2.00, Walgreens will ask you to buy another product to get the balance back into the positive. This ends up costing you more money because you

have to buy a product you did not plan for. Ensure that you never go into a negative balance.

3. When you are buying products at Walgreens using Register Rewards, you will want to buy products you normally use for less money.

Something else to remember is that when you are buying products, you can use your Register Rewards just before they expire to buy products you normally wouldn't buy and then give those products to others to help this. This is all about philanthropy and helping people in need. The Register Rewards will expire, and if you do not use them, they will be worthless. At least put them to good use by giving them to someone who may need them, or buy getting items someone else may need. For example, if you have lots of toothpaste, you can use the Register Rewards before they expire to get someone else some toothpaste, thereby saving them money.

Walgreens Coupon Strategy

What is the policy of Walgreens with coupons? Knowing what the policy is can help ensure you make the right choices when putting together a coupon strategy.

First, you are allowed to use a manufacturer coupon and Walgreens coupon on the same purchase but you can only use one of each and both coupons have to allow the use of the other.

If the manufacturer's coupon value is greater than the retail value of the product you are buying, you will not get cash back from the purchase from Walgreens. So, if you have a

Don't Throw Those Coupons Away!

manufacturer's coupon that says $5 off, while there is a sale that has the product only costing $3, you will not get $2 back. If the retail value is less than the value of the coupon, then two things can happen.

- The coupon value will be the retail value if the state requires taxes on the item.
- The coupon value will be the retail value plus taxes if the state does not require taxes to be paid on the item.

Naturally, you can only use the coupon during the time of the sale. As well, if there is no quantity limit on your Walgreens coupon, the manager of the Walgreens is completely within his right to put their own limit on it. This means that if you have a coupon that gives you 40 percent off toilet paper but does not say "Limit X Per Customer" on it, the manager can impose their own limit and say that no more than three can be bought per customer.

In regards to whether or not Walgreens will price match or accept coupons from another retailer like CVS or Rite Aid, it should be noted that Walgreens will not price match with other retailers. As well, Walgreens will not accept coupons from other retailers and they will not accept expired coupons.

If by some chance you purchase an item with a manufacturer's coupon and then want to return it, you will receive the retail price of the item back. So, if the retail price is $2.99 and the manufacturer coupon is $1.00 off, then the refund amount will be $2.99. However, if you return an item you bought with a Walgreens coupon, then you will receive the coupon price back. So, if the retail price is $3.99 and you use a Walgreens coupon of $1.00 off, then you get back $2.99, not $3.99.

One of the most common questions is if you have no limit on a coupon, and the coupon is a Buy One Get One Free coupon, how many times can you have that coupon scanned for the purchase? Walgreens has a policy that only one coupon can be used on a Buy One Get One Free because you are at the time only buying one coupon.

ExtraCare Bucks and the CVS Program

CVS is the second largest drug store chain in the United States, after the Walgreens drug store chain, with 7,001 stores in 45 states. Like Walgreens, CVS offers its own form of discounts that can offer you some big savings in your drug store shopping.

The ExtraCare Rewards program, also called Extra Care Bucks, allows you to earn money at any store or online when you use your ExtraCare card. With this card, you earn two percent back on every single purchase you make both in the store and online, and you get one Extra Buck on every two prescriptions that you purchase online and in-store with CVS.

There are other benefits that come with ExtraCare Rewards including:

1. Special offers are often printed on your store receipt when you are a member of the program.

Don't Throw Those Coupons Away!

2. You receive special savings when you are a part of the program and sign up for e-mail offers.

3. The more purchases you make on your ExtraCard, the more rewards that you will receive.

The Process to Saving Money with CVS

1. Join the program by filling out a brochure in the store, or visiting CVS.com.

2. When you go to the store, present your card at the time of your purchase and you will get two percent back on your purchase. Every three months, your receipt prints out your Extra Care Bucks.

3. Each time that you present your card when having your prescriptions filled, you get one Extra Care Buck for every two prescriptions that you fill out.

4. Each month, a savings booklet is sent out by CVS that offers Extra Care Bucks on certain items. When you buy these items at the store and present your card, the bucks print at the bottom of your receipt.

5. Every Extra Care Buck can be used on more purchases through CVS because they act like money. You can also combine your Extra Care Bucks with manufacturer coupons.

Some CVS Tips

1. Always bring your Extra Care Rewards card with you so that it can be scanned each time you make a purchase to give you extra rewards.

2. Check the monthly booklet that is sent out by CVS and ensure that you buy items that are free after Extra Care Bucks.

Don't Throw Those Coupons Away!

3. Make sure you pay attention to the Extra Care Bucks because there is expiration dates printed there. You do not want to let free money expire on you, otherwise you lose savings.

4. Keep an eye on the CVS weekly ads so you can see when there are additional savings. The monthly ad also has savings that you can use with the Extra Care program.

5. When you shop online, make sure you enter in your Extra Care card number on all CVS purchases at the CVS website.

6. Stack your Extra Care bucks with manufacturer coupons on sale days so that you can get the maximum savings.

7. Only two CVS coupons can be used per item, so be sure you do not expect to use more.

8. You do not have to fulfill the Extra Care promotions in just one transaction or only at one store. You can complete the promotional offer over time but just keep in mind the expiration date.

9. Filling out new or transferred prescriptions at CVS will usually get you a gift card that you can use at CVS on your purchases.

10. CVS will match prescription prices, so if you find a place that has cheaper prescriptions, have CVS match them and get more savings with your CVS gift card and Extra Care Bucks.

11. You can print off internet coupons from CVS and then use them in the store to get extra savings on your purchases.

12. Not all CVS stores honor Extra Care promotions as rain checks, so be sure to find out if your CVS store does.

13. Become a member of the CVS Advisor Panel. When you do this, which just involves filling out surveys, you can get Extra Care Bucks.

Don't Throw Those Coupons Away!

When you are shopping with CVS, you want to make sure that you put your CVS coupons to work with any sales that may be on at CVS. One example of this is to have a $10 coupon for products that are also on sale for $5 off. This gives you $15 off on the price, giving you even bigger savings.

One important thing to do with CVS coupons is to use as many as you can on a visit. The more CVS coupons you use, the more money you save and the more CVS coupons you get on your purchases for the next time you come in.

With this type of strategy where you are buying things you may not need at that point, you are stockpiling which is very important. Remember to stock up on items that are on sale, will not spoil and are things you need without a doubt, like toilet paper. It is possible to have a year's worth of toilet paper at your disposal by using CVS coupons when you have the chance.

In addition to having your CVS coupons at sales, you should also combine your CVS coupons with manufacturer coupons. Doing this can give you some major savings on your purchases. Remember, stacking coupons is a great strategy for grocery stores and it works just as well for drugstores. An example of this is if you have a $2 Off CVS coupon for toilet paper, and $4 Off manufacturer coupon from the toilet paper company. This gives you six dollars off on the purchase. If there is also a store sale that gives you 10 percent off the purchase, you end up saving even more.

Don't Throw Those Coupons Away!

CVS Coupons Online

CVS also offers a Clip and Print Coupon Center feature on www.cvs.com, which allows you to print and collect coupons that you can redeem at the CVS pharmacy near you. The coupons are for nearly everything that you could possibly want to buy at the store, and that provides you with a lot of savings. You can also put in your ZIP code to find local savings that you can take advantage o.

One great feature of the Clip and Print Coupon Center is that you can also print off manufacturer coupons at the center, as well as pharmacy-exclusive offers. In addition, you can even click "Spread the Word" so you can be notified by e-mail of new deals being offered through CVS.

Stockpiling With CVS Bonus-Package Deals

Once a year, CVS will run a program where they have a bonus-pack deals. These bonus packs provide you with a free pack of something, usually something like toilet paper, toothpaste, or shampoo, while at the same time giving you Extra Care Bucks to use. For something like toilet paper, it can be possible to stock up on a year's worth by using this bonus-pack deals.

1. Since you are starting out from scratch, you will want to start small. So, go out and buy two cheap items, usually around

Don't Throw Those Coupons Away!

four dollars each. By doing this, you get three Extra Care Bucks for each item you buy. Use a Buy One Get One Free coupon for the item. Now, you pay $3.99 and you get back six Extra Care Bucks because you bought two items.

2. Now, go back with your six Extra Care Bucks and buy four more of that same item using two Buy One Get One Free. Now, you have spent $6 and you receive back 12 Extra Care Bucks.

3. Continue doing this by doing one transaction per day at different CVS stores.

Remember with each coupon and offer, you want to reduce how much you buy, which you do by using CVS money and combining it with coupons and manufacturer coupons. You also want to try and continue rolling your Extra Care Bucks into more Extra Care Bucks by rolling them into deals like Buy One Get One Free.

Be sure to ask the cashiers what the coupon policy of the store is. You do this to make sure you do not make the store angry with your couponing strategy, but also because some stores allow expired CVS coupons to use.

Single Check Rebates and Rite Aid Program

Rite Aid is one of the largest drug store chains in the United States and it operates out of more than 4,900 stores in 31 states. Like Walgreens and CVS, it offers a program to help you save money when you are shopping with them.

Don't Throw Those Coupons Away!

The program works with Rite Aid offering special rebates on certain items. Each item that is part of this program will have a Single Check Rebate marking on it and you can actually visit Rite Aid's website to see what products are offered through the program. The website is https://riteaid.rebateplus.com and you can use this to make a shopping list of the items you want to save on.

When you go to the store, you buy the item that has been marked and you keep the receipt. Once you are home, go to Rite Aid's website. Once you do go to the website you can sign up for the Single Check Rebate account. In any given month-period, you can enter in your receipts to get your rebates totaled up and sent to you within two weeks.

The Step-By-Step Process

In order to understand how this product works, you can go through this step-by-step process, listed here in more detail than above.

1. Register with the Rite Aid Rebate website at http://www.riteaid.rebateplus.com and click on "Sign Up".
2. Enter in your email address and postal address so that you can receive your rebates in the mail.
3. Click on "View the Offers" so you can see the current offers offered through the company with the rebate program.

4. Ensure that you read the details of each offer very carefully because some special terms are on various offers. If Rite Aid has a rebate where you get five dollars back if you buy one bottle of shampoo and one bottle of conditioner, both by the same company, then you have to buy both products to get the rebate, not two shampoo bottles.

5. At the store, buy the products that have been listed within in the program. Once you get your receipt, hold onto it because you are going to need it in the next step.

6. Go to the Rite Aid website and sign into your account. Then, enter in your receipts putting in the information that is requested by the form on the website.

7. You will then receive an e-mail confirmation with the information you have entered.

8. A few days later, you will receive an e-mail from Rite Aid that explains you rebate has been processed and are available to receive in the mail.

9. At the end of the month, go to the website and make sure you have entered all your receipts and make sure your rebates have been processed.

10. Click on "Request a Check" at the end of each month. You can only do this once per month, but once you have done it you will receive a check that is sent to you from Rite Aid.

The Coupon Policy of Rite Aid

Understanding the coupon policy of a store can ensure you use your coupons to their fullest potential. This is no different with Rite Aid and their coupons. So, what is the coupon policy of Rite Aid?

Don't Throw Those Coupons Away!

1.   Rite Aid will accept four different types of coupons. They will accept coupons generated by manufacturers, coupons in the newspaper, manufacturer coupons in Rite Aid flyers, Rite Aid coupons and internet coupons that come from the Rite Aid website or are official Rite Aid coupons.

2.   Rite Aid does not honor coupons that have expired.

3.   If your coupon has been reproduced, altered or misused in any way, Rite Aid will not honor the coupon.

4.   Rite Aid has the right to deny the redemption of a coupon that may show signs of what is called misrepresentation.

Further Rite Aid Tips

Whenever you are using coupons on the Single Check Rebate, you will be bringing in money for yourself. The reason for this is that if you buy something that costs $4.99, and it has a $1 coupon on it, you will pay $3.99 when you are in the store. Once you submit the rebate to Rite Aid, you get $4.99. That means you just made money by using a coupon.

Whenever you are in the store, make sure you get the booklet that shows all the rebate items for that entire month. You can go through this booklet, which is free, and find items that you can get using your Rite Aid coupons.

For an advanced type of couponing with Rite Aid, you can do the following. When you are at the Rite Aid store, grab yourself a copy of the monthly booklet and find the rebate items in the book that you think may be free during that month. These are often the ones with certain dates only for the sale, or if there are stars next to the items.

Don't Throw Those Coupons Away!

Now, contact every single company listed within that booklet and request coupons from them. This allows you to get even more coupons for you to use when you want to save money at Rite Aid.

Further Information on Rite Aid

Of course, using Rite Aid does not stop there. There are some things to remember and understand if you are going to use the Rite Aid coupon system properly.

1.   First, you cannot have more than one Single Check Rebate account per household.
2.   If your receipt is not credited to your account, don't worry. If you wait you will eventually receive a check. If you do not want to wait, all you have to do is call 1-888-213-9920.
3.   You can use internet printable coupons, but you can only use one per transaction, or one per coupon type per transaction. Also, the value of the coupon cannot exceed five dollars.

If you go to the store and you find that something labeled as free under the Single Check Rebate is out of stock and there are no more of the item coming in before the end of the sale, just go and talk to the cashier and ask for a rain check. When you get your rain check, attach the picture and price from the weekly ad to the rain check. Now, while you wait for the item to be in stock, look for new coupons and check the stores on a weekly basis. Once the item does come into stock, go and buy it and make sure that you coupon says rain check on it. Also, you have

Don't Throw Those Coupons Away!

to ensure you buy the right item and that means the same size, color, brand, flavor and everything else.

Chapter Ten
Don't Throw It Away

Saving money is more important now than ever before. Throughout the United States, people are going through a deep recession that has many people tightening up their wallets in an effort to save money.

There are three ways that people are choosing to save money in this economy, but only one is a good idea.

1. Eating less
2. Eating poorer quality, and therefore cheaper, food
3. Using coupons

If you eat less, you are only hurting your body and your health, as well as the health of the people in your family. If you eat poor quality food just to save money, you are doing the exact same. Eating fast food instead of no food is an improvement, but not much of one because of the damage you are doing to your body.

So, how can you eat good food but save money?

The Power of Coupons

Well, if you have been reading this book you know the right answer, and the right answer is using coupons to buy the food you need without spending too much money in the process. With coupons, you greatly lower the amount you spend on your groceries and that is money you can put elsewhere in order to keep your bills low.

If you have lost employment, or your employment has been cut back, something like coupons will greatly assist you.

Think about it. If you usually spend $200 a week on groceries and you can lower that to $50 per week, while still maintaining the quality of food, you save $150 per week. That comes to $600 per month! Think of what you could do with that money. You are still eating the same amount that you did before, and you are able to spend that money on your bills, on gas, or just put it into savings. If you are putting it into savings, then using coupons are allowing you to put away $600 per month, or $7,200 per year.

Remember Your Coupon Strategy

It is amazing to think that you could save over $7,000 based on just using coupons.

Of course, it is not just enough to use coupons. You need to know how to use coupons and when you know how to use coupons, you can save even more money in your shopping.

Don't Throw Those Coupons Away!

If you go to the grocery store and just use coupons, you save maybe 20 to 30 percent on your savings. When you spend $200, that still amounts to savings of $40 to $60, but is that really enough?

You need to use coupon strategy to save money and that comes in many forms as you have seen, including:

• Combining coupons with sales in order to save extra money.
• Combining manufacturer coupons with store coupons.

These two coupon strategies are able to double your savings. Now we go from saving 20 to 30 percent to saving 40 to 60 percent and that means spending $80 to $120 less on the $200 you used to spend. All that money saved goes to your bank, to your bills, or to other expenses that you may have.

There is so much more to coupons than just clipping them out of the Sunday paper. As you have seen in this book, coupons come in many different forms and they come from many different sources.

If you only try and get coupons from the Sunday paper, you are doing yourself a disservice. These days, places like the internet have opened up where you can get coupons from and has created a wonderland of coupons for you.

In addition, more and more companies are now offering coupons from other companies. These companies make their living by having you sign up for their coupon service. They get you the coupons and you pay them for the time.

Even if you don't get coupons through here, you can get coupons from old sources like coupon trains, and new sources like eBay. The number of places you can get coupons from has grown immeasurably and with every growth of the availability of coupons, the possibility of savings grows for you.

Coupons Make Life Easy

Coupons are a wonderful thing that makes life easy for all of us. When you have coupons to use, you are essentially using free money because coupons are money. When you have a coupon that saves you four dollars, then it is like the store giving you four dollars to use. Every dollar that a coupon saves you is a dollar that stays in your wallet and in tough economic times that is incredibly important.

Coupons for Every Purchase

Of course, coupons are not just for grocery stores. In fact, nearly every major company on Earth offers coupons on everything from a loaf of bread to a 50-inch high definition plasma television. Even when you need to stay healthy, you can get coupons.

Coupons come in a variety of forms, but they all do one thing and that is save us money.

www.ingramcontent.com/pod-product-compliance
Lightning Source LLC
Chambersburg PA
CBHW060417050426
42449CB00009B/1999